Viral Cat

Spring 2014 Issue

Edited by Tiffany Slotwinski

ISBN: 0615976107
ISBN-13: 978-0615976105

Printed in the United States.

LETTER FROM THE EDITOR

Dear Readers,

The content found in Viral Cat continues to ping through cyber space, true to its name. Since 2008, Viral Cat has worked hard to develop a space where screenwriters, photographers, and comic book artists could have their work presented alongside poets, painters, and videographers.

The Spring 2014 Issue of Viral Cat encourages readers to think about potential—what does it mean for someone to have potential, and what does it mean for potential to be lost? Can potential ever be lost or gained, or does the term merely suggest an absence of some other quality? A special thanks to all who have made Viral Cat possible through submissions and donations.

If you like what you see, be sure to check us out on the web at www.viralcat.com. Donations are welcome! If you would like to submit your work for consideration in our next issue, please send your submissions to viralcatzine@gmail.com.

Viral Cat also accepts full-length manuscript submissions at viralcatpress@gmail.com. Please visit our website to view our published works.

Enjoy the immense talent of our contributors.

Tiffany Slotwinski
Editor-in-Chief, Viral Cat Press
www.viralcat.com

CONTENTS

the poet in wartime

by Christopher Mulrooney

her cigarette is lit still she asks for a match
just when he's about to light a firecracker to drop over the precipice

the news correspondent explains on his large map the divisions around
the city and the fighting there

she leaps and not to him but past him to an officer for succor
yes that is how it must seem to some in the circumstances

Somerset House / London, UK

by Sarah Kayss

Cardiff / Whales, UK

by Sarah Kayss

Regarding Rooms

by Marilyn Joy

You look into a room
to know it,
to find the corners,
walk the pale yellow walls
with your eyes—the frame
that holds a landscape,
an odd mirror, a cluster
of photographs, and
on the table
wild lavender stems and
tulips—red bells leaning in
a curved bend.
It's the way to feel safe, to
know a place,
see how the light lifts
against the curtains,
how the worn wood floor
feels under your feet.
It's like that when you
meet someone,
you look inside for these
smooth walls, for
safe corners, and behind
their eyes to see
where the light leans in.

J'adore le coup des fourmis, 2012
Die Schraube und der Bauer, 2012
by Samy Sfoggia

A Birth in the War Zone

by John Grey

A mental scream busts free,
a boy, newly born in blood
AK47's lie awake under pillows,
tank and gunpowder congealed,
and a prayer fisted by a shiftless priest
arrived too early, the ambulances humming
as long as one tooth can grind another,
as the piano cries, alive, alive,
echoing down hospital corridors
But the taxi-driver ate his last fare,
dissolved like sugar,.
frost and chill, soup and pot,
frozen bells chiming, no ringing coda,
love grated down to a dust
on the heartless pestle,
in the poems about candy machines,
or the blue shawl of a father's lover.
no rest for the dead,
or the woolens, or the clocks,
or money, that ancient champion,
for which the tubercular cripple grasps.
Pennies fell down as ears were deafened,
pennies that sounded like a dense city street,
perished and froze and pushing against the wall
seething from bony needles
shellac, the nurse's flower, speaking, laughing,
that anyone would pay three cents
in leaden, hanging-tree dawn
to see another baby born.
The message gasps through an army of chills,
the body wants more to drink -
the whore gives birth,, propped inside her mini-dress

as time throws up in the bucket,
then pumps with milk, chatters about teats.
towards evening and a car homeward bound.
Then when they shouted names and sexes,
their cheeks froze, bodies shook, tears danced
painfully like raw toes on rough-hide rocks.

Rain, oil on linen

by Dagmar Hrickova

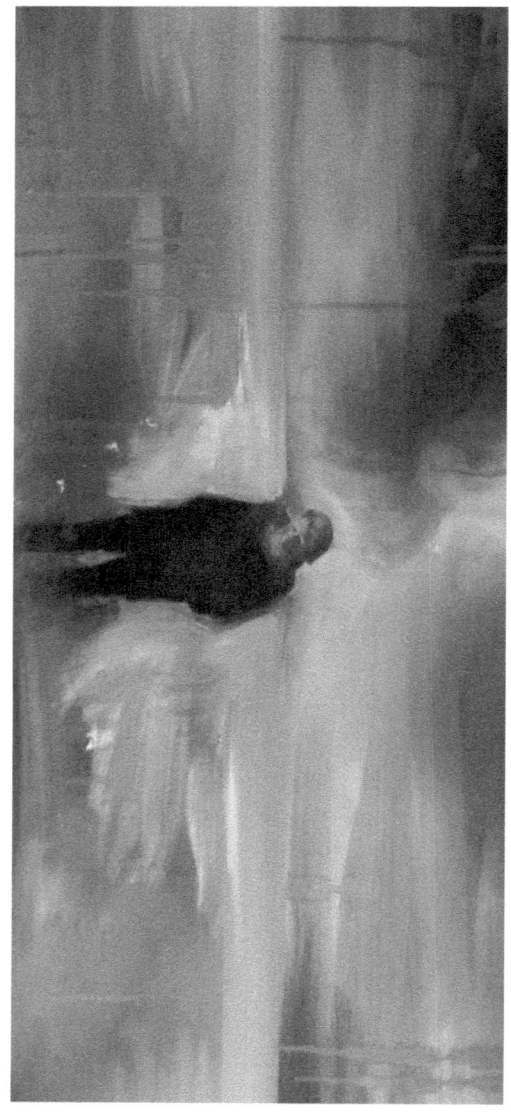

A Word ... My Kingdom for a Word

by Marilyn Joy

Some babies are born
a few good grunts and there they wail,
demanding the world
bow down to them.
Others have to be pulled, pried, cut out.
Sleepy-eyed and yawning
they look around and wonder why
they were yanked from their aquatic
world inside the womb.

Words are like that, some arriving slick,
easy, not weighted with
the labor of indecision, of hesitation.
Others argue with their order
or cling willful to the tip of your tongue,
hang out with impossible friends
that taint
their reputation and reliability.

I used to think the ones that came easily,
not out of my head or history,
were the bright stars—lithe spontaneous
sparks that could lead the parade.
But have come to know
the merit of my prodigal sons,

hard-won words, worried over,
awakened in the night over,
when they finally arrive—repentant and
resplendent souls,
it takes the breath and emboldens
a pen to strive, to labor long
with these reluctant, ineffable utterances.

Catechuman Waiting Baptism on Easter Eve

by Tinca Veerman

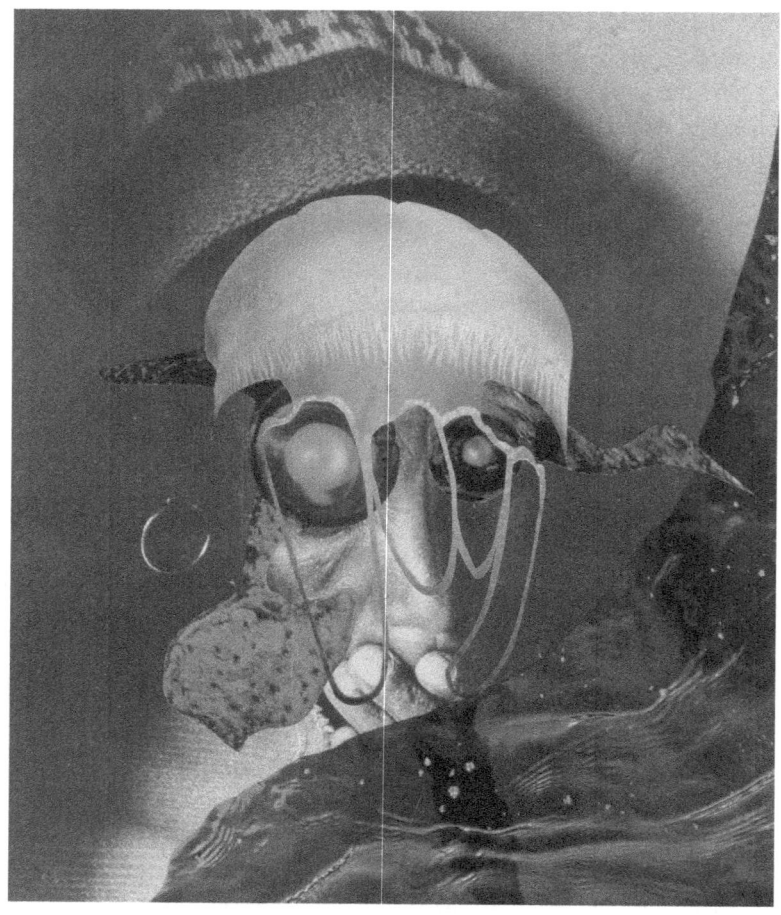

In the Bleak Midwinter

by Marilyn Joy

> *In the bleak midwinter*
> *Frosty wind made moan,*
> *Earth stood hard as iron,*
> *Water like a stone… Christina Rossetti*

No moon. The light let through the blinds
must mean morning.
Barely closed my eyes and another day appears
like a mantra with no words—silence
so faint, so fragile
it dissolves
amid plans and lists and arguments
with the dark days

that find my feet on the floor
as I remember my age and my mistakes
and wonder how I might hold onto this day,
how I might make it count for something.
But eating breakfast I'm caught in thought
and swallow down the morning light without
ever tasting its sweetness,

where I hold this dilemma in my hand
like the smooth striated stone found on a beach
under an inch of receding wave—
surprising colors flying from its hard face
wet with thirst for the sun.
Later, out of my pocket, it was muted, ordinary,
like the countless stones crowding
sand against the cliffs.

McGillicuddy's Wake

by Donal Mahoney

Two new crutches and two double shots of Bushmills Irish Whiskey enabled Joe Faherty to move from the back seat of Moira Murphy's 1976 Buick into Eagan's Funeral Home for Tim McGillicuddy's wake. At 87, Joe was in bad shape, only a tad better than McGillicuddy who looked splendid in a rococo casket.

The way the funeral home had painted McGillicuddy's face, he looked better than most of the folks who had come to say good-bye. Many of them were in their eighties. Even Moira, who still had her driver's license, was creaky at 75.

McGillicuddy was 90 when he fell off his horse out in the country. Until that moment he hadn't been sick a day in his life. Never drank and never smoked. Women were his passion. He was was calling on a couple until the day he died.

Few folks knew that McGillicuddy had been expelled from Ireland by the British in 1920. He was 18. He had been captured at 16 bringing guns to older IRA rebels who were fighting the British. A few rebels with rifles caused the British occupiers a lot of problems.

For two years they kept McGillicudy in prison. They finally agreed to let him go to America. Why not, McGillicuddy thought. Life in America had to be better than prison.

In the funeral home, however, much to the disgust of Joe Faherty, the priest had come to the wake early. This meant Joe didn't have time to grab his crutches and get to the bar next door before the priest started the rosary. The custom at Irish wakes was that the priest would arrive at 6:30 p.m. and all the men would have made it to the bar by then. The women would say the rosary with the priest.

But this was a new priest and there he was in front of the casket saying 15 decades of the rosary. Not the traditional five, as was the case at Polish wakes.

Joe figured it would take the priest an hour to finish. Then he'd ask Moira to take him home. He was too tired to go to the bar. Besides, he had had more than the two double shots of Bushmills he had mentioned to Moira.

Moira drove Joe home. She waited until he was inside the house. She wanted to make certain his new crutches wouldn't result in a fall. Joe waved good-bye to Moira and shut the door but didn't lock it. He had to let the dog out.

Although he hated to turn on a light--he lived on Social Security-- he turned on just one because it was as dark inside as it was outside. He planned to buy some candles.

As soon as Joe turned on the light, he saw McGillicuddy in his favorite recliner wearing the same fancy suit he had on in the casket.

"What the hell are you doing here," Faherty asked. "Why didn't you stay where you were. We got through the rosary so why do this. They'll come here first, considering all the years we've been friends."

McGillicuddy didn't say a word.

"Well," said Faherty, "if you aren't in the mood to talk, I'll have another Bushmills till you decide to say something. You don't look dead. In fact, you never looked better."

McGillicuddy maintained his silence.

"It's too bad you don't drink. You could join me in some Bushmills. It's as good today as it was back in Ireland."

Down deep Faherty didn't know what to do with dead McGillicuddy in his favorite recliner. How long, he wondered, would McGillicuddy stay. He wanted to be friendly but there was a limit to his hospitality.

"Let's watch the news on television," Faherty said, turning on the set. "Maybe they'll explain how I've come to enjoy your company.

"You didn't drive, did you? If you need a lift I'm sure Moira will come pick you up. After all, you two almost got married. I think she's still fond of you."

Still, not a word out of McGillicuddy.

"I'm going in the kitchen and call Moira," Joe said. "I'll be right back. We can talk about which way you're going, up or down, if you know what I mean.

"The bets were about even on you. I told everyone you'd be in heaven before they embalmed you. Except for the women, you probably didn't commit another mortal sin in your life. Of course, you were dead when the priest gave you the Last Rites. Don't know if they work on a dead person. Let's hope they do."

Faherty hoisted himself out of the guest chair, got on his crutches and headed for the kitchen to call Moira. He stumbled a bit on the rug because he wasn't used to the crutches or all that Bushmills.

"Hello, Moira," Faherty said when she answered the phone. "Could you drop back here for a minute. I've got an unexpected guest who needs a lift. I think you'll be happy to see him. I have to go to bed. We've got McGillicuddy's funeral Mass tomorrow. Wouldn't want to miss that."

Moira said she'd be right over. Faherty, heading back to the parlor, tripped over his dachshund. The dog had slept through all the commotion with McGillicuddy. Joe landed with a thud on his forehead. He never moved.

The next day Moira blamed Joe's death on his crutches and indeed that was part of the problem. No mention was made of the Bushmills, however. Moira, who had found the body, found the half empty bottle and took it home.

As Joe's driver for three years Moira thought she deserved the liquor. But she wondered who the guest was that Joe had called about. When she got to his house, there was only the dachshund snoring next to the body.

At Fifteen, Visiting My Uncle Frank

by John Grey

Preserve, he says, though why I don't know
Preserve books no one reads.
And farm implements from the twenties.
Letters from dead people.
Post cards from the living.

He shows me to his room
where a hundred butterflies are pinned behind glass.
This is the rarest in my collection,
he says, pointing to an insect with purple wings.
It's no more common
for me having seen its corpse.

In a cabinet in the cellar,
he's stored a hundred empty beer cans
representing fifty seven countries
some of which no longer exist.

And then there's his great grandfather's pipe,
weaving loom, bottle tops, horse shoe
and the sheet music to "Be My Love."

And wouldn't you know,
on my way home,
a pretty blonde girl smiles at me.
Ephemeral, half-meant...
I'll keep it.

Chelsea Market 2

by Jeff Williamson

14 days' furlough

by Christopher Mulrooney

oh what a mass of time we do have here
the on-and-off patrols who needs them
and the guard duty these are a few rounds of the clock
the sun is shining moon and stars around these hours

Gypsy

by M. Krochmalnik Grabois

My lover rides her bike fast
through the wind and rain

Her head is shaved on one side
the hair on the other is jet black
and hangs long
now wet and stringy

Rain beads on her bright red lips
as on a car recently polished
Her eyes are black
She grips the handlebars tight
and pedals hard

She wears a blood red scarf
and looks like a gypsy
who lives in a camp
behind a stark apartment building
in Salamanca Spain
home of the Pontifical University
whose power she neutralizes with evil intent

On her forearm is a tattoo
a symbol she designed herself
a planet spinning anarchically
Next to the symbol are words
in no language known to man
Though she tells me they are Portuguese
I know they're not

She pedals fast
through wind and rain

Orange Cat

by John Kaniecki

I saw her not as before
Not the well groomed feline
Sweetly purring at my door

Cast out from home
Abandoned to roam
A feat hard for a street savvy cat
Let alone, one who has known
Comfort and only that

No winter's bitter freezing snow
No hunger or soaking rain
No wandering to and fro
With anxious worried pain

So I contemplated
The Sahara and lands far away
And I hated
The evil they
Experience
It makes not sense
Babies die of starvation
While others live in crowded slums
And when they strive for salvation
The horror of war comes

So I left my refuge secure
And fed her milk in a bowl
I could do no more
Except mourn in my soul

The Medicine Man

by Tinca Veerman

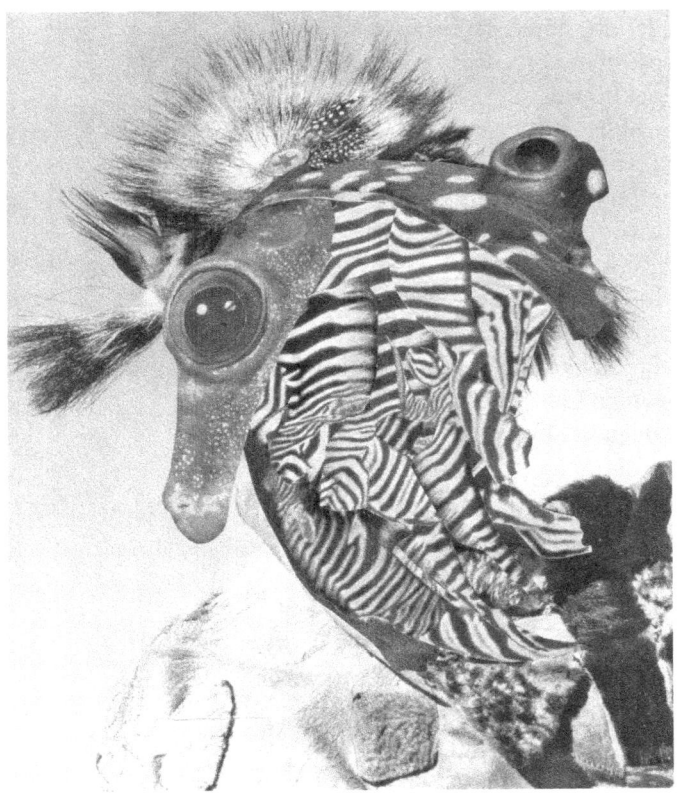

Experimental Poetry

by John Kaniecki

In ballerina choreographed grace
She spread her bare legs creating an obtuse angle
Leering, peering on
Identical Jack O' Lantern grins on every face
Soiled white jackets sadistic serial killers and worse
Dissecting, bisecting all in the name of science
The unwittingly ignorant subject
A funky, junky, cosmic monkey
In palm of hand a seven dimensional round peg
Attempting to put it into a two dimensional square
Nothing in nature occurs naturally with four even sides
Right Allen Ginsburg?
Draconian demonology dictates drastic demands
Reaganomics!
A non existent government is the best
Antithesis of anarchy
Corporate wage slavery, buyer beware
Recite the lines perfectly fine puppet
Alzheimer's progressed beyond the point of no return
But the red button is no movie prop
Neither is the primate with wires infesting his cranium's moist soft
insides
Envious eyes fall on Doctor Mengele
"He had real freedom"
"How can we benefit mankind so hampered?"
The pimping PhD's are seriously somber
Not knowing the irony
Or the reality
Technology simply complicates
Right Johnny Africa!?!

from the editorial offices

by Christopher Mulrooney

it has come to our attention that certain authors are making light of
our little effort here
this will cease as of 0800 hours
any scribe found to be in violation of this order will be shot
and we don't mean with Mark Twain's popgun either

Emmy Body Paint 11

body paint by Israel Morales; photography by Angel Velazquez

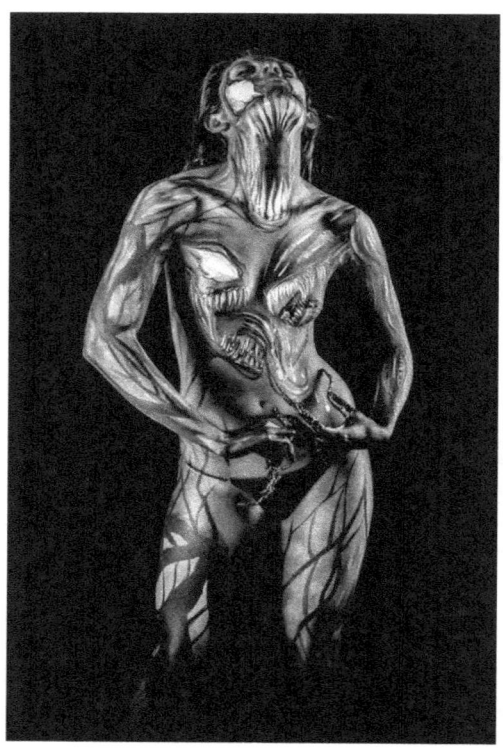

Kevin Loves Lisa

by Ally Malinenko

This is what it says on the metal door of the bathroom stall:
Kevin
Loves
Lisa,
with a little heart for emphasis.

Next to that it says,
Shane and Mary forever.

And above that,
Matthew and Marie equals destiny.

I couldn't help but enjoy the rhyme scheme on that one
as I sat there, peeing out the four beers
we'd already had in this tourist trap
of a bar on the San Francisco wharf
because we were too tired
after hitching a ride back
over the Golden Gate bridge
from a Scottish man driving
a tourist trolley
who said the company charges 35 a piece
but he'd take both of us for 15
as long as we had cash—

we did—

and don't mind the stopover in Sausalito—

we didn't.

And now here I am,
too tired to walk back up to North Beach,
reading the graffiti in the women's room stall
all about love.

I never have a pen on me
let alone a sharpie
to doodle
my thoughts on the metal doors of bar restrooms,
probably because I don't carry a purse,
but other people do,
because I am never without reading material.

I wonder about these women,
the ink at their fingertips,
the truth of their heart
and minds ready to become a permanent part
of the bar landscape,
and I can't help but think,
that's it?
That's all they have to say is
that Kevin loves them?
Not even that they love Kevin.
No, the order is important.
Kevin Loves Lisa forever and ever and ever.

This is the most we can muster, women?
Really?

Because back in New York City,
which feels so far from here,
and back in time
farther still,
someone once scribbled

You're drunk Kerouac go home,
in the men's room stall of the White Horse,

which as far as graffiti goes, is pretty damn good.
And I can't help but wonder
what else we can write besides
Kevin Loves Lisa,
which of course
I'm sure he does
or did
at the moment Lisa pulled from her bag
a sharpie and sealed their future on this door.

And I wonder is it the beer
or the chocolate-tinis that stifles our pen?
That stays our tongue?
That reduces us to nothing more than
Kevin Loves Lisa.
Not even Lisa Loves Kevin
because we all know
to be loved
is better than to love.

No one writes poems on the walls of this bar
but I've seen a few in the Grassroots
and once an amazing doodle
on the side of a piano
which shared the bathroom space
in New Orleans.

No, on this door,
it is love and only love that we want to talk about,
that Lisa and Marie and Mary,
three women who I now picture together
here in this stall,
giggling
brave on vanilla flavored shots,

breaking the rules
in their first big girls weekend
trip to San Francisco.

And suddenly, while peeing,
I hate these girls.
I hate them for not being poets,
for reducing themselves
to nothing but their relationships

as if couple-dom is the ultimate
status update.

I hate these girls for having nothing
in their empty little heads and empty
little hearts
but to declare
that they have something
that you don't.
They have a love,
who loves them
all the time and don't you doubt
it cause that's why they wrote it in permanent ink.

I'm being harsh, I know,
as I ball up the toilet paper and wipe and flush
and wash my hands and return to the bar
to ask my husband
what men write about on the walls of
their stalls

because it has to be better
than what we women got going and I'm starting
to think that the war of the sexes
will never end if we keep
ratcheting up the bulllshit quota
by deciding to limit ourselves

to the two names between the ampersand,
to define ourselves by the fingers entwined
or not entwined in ours.

I want to find Lisa and shake her
and ask her what she thought the day
she saw her mother crying at the kitchen table
or what she thought
the first time she heard a record skip.
Did she believe with all her heart that this moment
was never going to be the same?

Plus
I want to know what Kevin thinks,
what he writes on the stall doors,
so I ask my husband who cocks an eyebrow
because it seems that I'm always
asking these sort of things
and I wonder if that too
is getting tiring.

What do they write on the stalls, I ask,
as he pulls on his beer and glances
at the playoff game over the bar,
knowing he's secretly rooting for the Dodgers
even though we're in Giants country,
and he says
it's mostly about getting head.
Or getting laid.
Or getting some.

And I sigh
and drink my beer
and think
maybe it doesn't matter
maybe I'm just an old married woman
who doesn't remember what it's like

to want to tell the whole world
about how great Kevin is.
And maybe he is,
even if he did write that thing
about getting head on the bathroom wall
of his stall
which I hope, for Lisa's sake isn't about her.

And then I think
I hope that I won't have to pee again
before we get up the hill to Broadway
and Columbus
to have a dark and stormy at Vesuvio.

Wondering What the Future Will Bring, oil on linen

by Dagmar Hrickova

Hot and Cold

by John Grey

The porridge is hot
and outside is so searing
that the lawn
is brown as toast,
and the water boiling
for the coffee's so hot
that she can't leave her
hand more than a second
in its steam
and he just damns its whistle,
damns its shrill intrusion
in his newspaper world,
where the weather is hot,
the whole of Illinois is hot,
there's even news of hot times
in other hot places,
and the Cubs are hot,
the Cubs are hotter than
a hot streak;
how'd you sleep,
she asks;
it was hot,
he replies;
but those sheets were
cold as winter nights,
and her body was so cold
it was as if she'd been waked,
but he was cold anyhow,
cold as chicken pieces
in the freezer,
cold as the Cubs in September,
or the wind from Canada;

of course it's hot...
the sun's like a furnace;
but hell it's cold...
a whole other world.
no sun in its sky.

Wheelchair

by M. Krochmalnik Grabois

Her husband is a quadriplegic
so alongside her Capezio sticker
on their van's bumper
I'd rather be dancing
is his handicapped sticker
a blue wheelchair

In the kitchen he drinks vodka
occasionally gives a sip to his old Airedale
the stinkiest dog in the South

She comes in to make dinner
and he tells her that he's going to create
a new kind of zoo
one inhabited solely
by different varieties of snails and slugs
He's going to get
the largest banana slugs known to man
and show them in black light

She says: no one will come to a zoo like that
People want to see animals moving around

Slugs and snails move around, he protests
only slowly

They get into an argument
which turns violent
Drunken and diabolic
he powers his wheel chair into her legs
runs over her feet
In pain she falls to the floor

and he bashes her body
with his foot rests

She calls the police
but they refuse to arrest him
The neighbors up and down the street
see the squad car
and go: *tut tut*
That awful woman is abusing
 that nice paralyzed man
again

Gabbia Di Volo, 2012

by Samy Sfoggia

Barbara the Clown

by Sayuri Yamada

Barbara the clown came to the party.
Her right side was red. Her left side was white.
Her right-side plaited hair was red. Her right-side face was red. Her right-side baggy costume was red. Her right shoe was red.
Her left-side plaited hair was white. Her left-side face was white.
Her right-side baggy costume was white. Her left shoe was white.

Only her hat sitting on the top of her head was all white.
Only her eyes were all brown.

Her red part wasn't arty. Her white part wasn't smarty.
But Richard was pleased. It was his party.
But it wasn't a hen party. It wasn't a tea party. It wasn't a search party. It wasn't a third party. It was his birthday party!

He was happy happy happy.
His friends were happy happy happy.
Their mothers were happy happy happy.

Barbara the clown danced.
Her red plait pranced. Her white plait pounced.
She was so funny.
The sky was so sunny.
Richard was a happy sonny.
All the kids and all the mothers laughed at Barbara.

Barbara produced a pigeon from her red sleeve. Secretly, she heaved a sigh of relief.

It wasn't because she didn't make people pale. It wasn't because she didn't prevail. It wasn't because she didn't wail. It was because she didn't fail!

Kids clapped their hands. Mothers had become her fans.
"It is the best birthday party," Richard screamed.
"You are the best birthday boy." She beamed.
The sky was blue, the leaves were green.
The candles had been blown, the cake had been eaten.

"Can you become a kitten?" Richard asked.
"Yes, I can." Barbara the clown unmasked.
From under her red-and-white face, a yellow kitten's face appeared.
Then she stripped off her outfit.
From under her red-and-white costume, a yellow kitten's body
appeared. Again he liked it.

Barbara the kitten danced and sang. All the kids danced and sang.
All the mothers danced and sang.

They were all happy, happy, happy.

Then Barbara the kitten slipped and fell down.
Kids stopped dancing and singing.
Mothers stopped dancing and singing.
From under her kitten's body, a voice rose, "Help me."
Kids heard the voice.
Mothers heard the voice.
When Barbara the kitten stood up, Jason was flattened on the
ground.

"Oh, Jason." Jason's mother crouched by him and checked if he had
a wound.

There was no wound!

Jason's mother smiled. Jason smiled. Other kids smiled. Other
mothers smiled. Barbara the kitten smiled.

"Can you be a snake?" Richard asked.
"Yes, I can." Barbara the kitten unmasked.

From under her yellow face, a green python's face appeared. Then she striped off her outfit.
From under her yellow body, a green python's body appeared. Again he liked it.

Barbara the python slithered and sang. All the kids slithered and sang. All the mothers slithered and sang.

They were all happy, happy, happy.

Then Barbara the python swallowed Tom.
Kids stopped slithering and singing.
Mothers stopped slithering and dancing.
From inside her tummy, a voice rose, "Not me."

Kids heard the voice.
Mothers heard the voice.

Tom's mothers said, "Not Tom."
Richard's mother said, "It should've been Richard."
Barbara the python said, "Sorry," and swallowed Richard.

From inside her tummy, two voices rose, "Hello, Tom," "Hello, Richard."

Richard's mother smiled. Tom's mother smiled. Kids smiled. Other mothers smiled. Barbara the python smiled.

It was a great birthday party.

Nikki

by Michael Lee Johnson

Watching doves
peck away,
all day long at
a full bowl
of mixed seeds,
out on the balcony
of my condo,
my cat curls
up on the sofa,
after a meager
meal of house flies-
and dreams of
sparrows with
wide soaring
wings.

Plant More Trees

by Benjamin Blake

She went away to college
And I just sat at home
Reading prose and poetry
And learning more than she was

Her hair transformed into a bird's nest
I cut mine short back and sides
She marched in abortion protests
While I just walked my dog

She found a new guy
One without a razor or shoes
I made out with the neighbors' daughter
In the woods behind my house

For all the picket waving
And chaining herself to trees
I can still name most species
By their bark and fallen leaves
And I doubt she knows the difference
Between a sycamore and a beech

Emmy Body Paint, 21

body paint by Israel Morales; photography by Angel Velazquez

Bi-Coastal
(screenplay excerpt)

written by Richard A. Lasser

"BI-COASTAL" is a feature-length screenplay by Richard Lasser.

Richard Lasser is an award-winning screenwriter whose film credits include "The Chosen Few," a feature-length psychological thriller produced by I VU Pictures, "The Counting House," a feature-length psychological horror produced by RAI Cinema, and ""Tricks of Love," a feature-length romantic comedy produced by Mutressa Movies, among others.

FADE IN:

INT. MANHATTAN, UPPER EAST SIDE, MAY LEE'S PENTHOUSE
APARTMENT - SUNSET

MAY LEE, 35, an elegant, Asian-American greyhound, is at
the top -- literally. From her Fifth Avenue penthouse
windows, Central Park and the West Side stretch out toward
the orange sky.

She's cosseted in her Architectural Digest furnishings,
embraced by her Chanel suit. You can almost smell her Clive
Christian $2000 bergamot and lime perfume.

She is alone. She sits on her sofa, sips a martini, reads
letters.

> CARRIE WILSON (V.O.)
> Dear Mrs. Lee, Ever since my
> chemotherapy, I've been so
> embarrassed to go out -- or even
> let my husband see me. But today,
> for the first time in so many
> years, I am happy.

While May reads the letter, we see an image of CARRIE
WILSON, 30s, painfully thin and bald, dressed in black,
sitting before a mirror in a black room. It seems as though
her bald head floats in space.

May comes up behind her, places a beautiful wig on her head
—transforms the woman from Ugly Duckling to Beautiful Swan.

> CARRIE WILSON (V.O.)
> With the new wig I feel alive
> again. I feel like a woman again.
> Thank you, Ms. Lee, so very much,
> Carrie Wilson.

May picks up another letter, reads.

> MARY JANE POTTER (V.O.)
> Dearest May, The wig is so
> beautiful. It looks just like my
> real hair used to.

We see an image of MARY JANE POTTER, 50s, dowdy and bald,
dressed in black, sitting before a mirror in a black room.
It seems as though her bald head floats in space.

All the age spots and imperfections in her sagging, lined
face are exaggerated by the lack of hair.

May comes up behind her, places a beautiful wig on her
head, tugs it this way and that -- transforms her from
grotesque to radiant.

                 MARY JANE POTTER (V.O.)
       I thought I was going to die when
       I got my diagnosis. And maybe I
       will. But at least I feel
       beautiful again. And it is all
       because of you. You are a godsend.
       Love, Mary.

May pours another martini, takes a drink. She picks up a
third letter.

                 JUDY KING (V.O.)
       Dear Ms. Lee, May God Bless you for
       your kindness and understanding.
       Because of you I went from being
       hysterical and not wanting to have
       my husband touch me, to confident
       and happy again. My husband kind
       of likes me now without the rug,
       but I feel better with the new
       drapes.

We see an image of Judy King, African-American, dressed in
black, sitting before a mirror in a black room.

It seems as though her bald head floats in space -- almost
like a chocolate malted milk ball. She's 40-ish, obese,
with a couple of double chins.

May comes up from behind her, places a wig on her head,
changes her from Mr. T. to Hallie Berry -- well, not quite.

But Judy is ecstatic.

                 JUDY KING (V.O.)
       It's all because of you. Do you
       know what an angel you are? I do.
       In His Name, Judy King.

May picks up another letter, this one in a business
envelope. It's from the IRS.

She takes out the letter, which she's obviously read many
times.

                 AUDITOR (V.O.)
       Dear Ms. Lee: The Internal Revenue
       Service is conducting an audit of
       your 2001 Federal Tax Return.
          (MORE)

                    AUDITOR (V.O.) (CONT'D)
          Based on your previous years' tax
          returns, we estimate that you
          should owe approximately four
          hundred ninety thousand, six
          hundred dollars in Federal Income
          Tax plus possible interest and
          penalties. You are requested to
          bring any and all records and
          documentation to justify your
          expenses and income on your 2010
          Return to the Internal Revenue
          Office at two p.m., Wednesday, June
          11...

She lowers the letter. Her elegant, reserved demeanor
dissolves into one of panic, fear.

She opens a bottle of pills, pops one.

                                                CUT TO:
INT. QUEENS, METHODIST CHURCH - MORNING

A joyous choir sings to the congregation in a church that
has seen better days.

The sweetest voice seems to belong to sunny KATHY MURCER,
20s.

Sunny, yes, but if you look deep into her eyes you see
storm clouds. She wears her long, blonde hair proudly --
and like her clothes -- conservatively.

Other members of the choir look to Kathy, smile at her. She
returns their appreciative looks with a modest smile that
warms them all.

Lonely-looking WALTER WRIGHT, 30s, choir leader, keeps one
eye on his hymn, one eye on Kathy.

INT. BINGO HALL - LATER

The dingy room is filled with SENIORS hunched over
partially-filled bingo cards, the game in progress.

Walter is at the front of the room next to a hopper full of
balls.

                    WALTER
          O.K. We ready for the next one?

                    SENIORS
          Ready!

Kathy circulates among the Seniors. Walter watches her as
he absently takes the next ball from the hopper.

                    WALTER
          I-forty-five. I-forty-five.

Kathy helps BARBARA MITCHELL, 70s, place her tile on her
card.

                    KATHY
          One more and you get Bingo!

                    BARBARA
          I just want you to know...well,
          all of us...

Barbara looks up and down the row. All the Seniors nod
affirmatively.

                    BARBARA (CONT'D)
          ...Want you to know how much we
          appreciate you.

Kathy smiles, but the look on her face seems to say she
doesn't deserve the praise.

INT. COMMUNITY HALL -- LATER

FAMILIES mill around, laugh, enjoy each other's company and
the steam table food.

Kathy sits in a corner alone, nibbles self-consciously.
Walter makes a tentative move in her direction. Kathy's
early warning radar picks up the blip and she gets up, moves
farther away.

PASTOR CONDEN approaches, sits next to her, perhaps a bit
too close for Kathy, who inches away.

                    PASTOR CONDEN
          Hey there.

                    KATHY
          Hello, Pastor. I should have the
          books done by next Sunday.

                    PASTOR CONDEN
          Kathy, you do so much for the
          church. Thank you for everything.

                    KATHY
          I'm going to organize a rummage
          sale. First Presbyterian raised
          four thousand dollars with theirs.
          I just know we can hit our goal if
          we try enough things.

                    PASTOR CONDEN
          Good Lord, Kathy. You're a one-
          woman fund raising machine.
          Between all you do for the church
          and your bookkeeping, when do you
          have time for yourself.

Walter comes over.

                    WALTER
          Hey, Pastor, that's what I'd like
          to know.

                    KATHY
          Oh, I have plenty of time. Matter
          of fact, I better get home. I've
          got some girls coming over to play
          cards.

                    WALTER
          Need an extra hand?

                    KATHY
          Don't think so, Walter. We need
          our girl talk time. You know.

                    PASTOR CONDEN
          I'll leave you two.

                    WALTER
          What about tomorrow night?

                    KATHY
          I, well....Sure, I guess I could.
          Why not?

                    WALTER
          Great! Eight o'clock O.K.?

                    KATHY
          Sure.

INT. KATHY MURCER'S APARTMENT - LATER

A modest apartment filled with happy, well-tended plants
and a bubbling fish tank.

A deck of cards sits on a card table.

Pictures of a younger Kathy with a young man in nature
scenes hang on the walls. Captions identify the locales:
"Benedict and me -- Appalachian Trail", "Yellowstone",
"Yosemite", etc.

There are some captions with empty spaces above them:
"Grand Canyon, St. Louis Gateway Arch."

Kathy, in the same clothes she wore at church, feeds the
fish.

                    KATHY
          Come here, Donner. Blitzen, come
          out from that grotto. It's dinner
          time.

Fish swim to the surface to feed. They touch her fingers,
with what actually seems like affection. Kathy blows them a
kiss.

                    KATHY(CONT'D)
          My good little fishies. I love
          you.

Kathy turns on the TV, tunes it to a reality dating show.
She sits at the card table, plays solitaire. She pops M and
Ms from a large bowlful on the table.

She takes out her day planner, opens it to the next day.
The evening is wide open.

She picks up the phone, dials.

                    KATHY (CONT'D)
          Hey, Walter.... No, we're taking a
          break right now....When I got home
          I realized I've got a client
          tomorrow night....Yeah, I'm sorry,
          too....

She closes the planner, continues the conversation -- if
you can call it that.

                    KATHY (CONT'D)
          Let's see. Wednesday....Nope, I'm
          booked then, too.... yeah, see
          you
          at choir practice.

INT. KATHY'S APARTMENT - MORNING

Spreadsheets on the desk, Kathy types on her computer, talks into the phone cradled on her shoulder.

> KATHY
> Yes, Ms. Ortiz....I'll bring everything in a couple of hours.... Don't you worry.... I'm not quite done, but it looks like you're getting a refund....I know. Isn't that great?....No, don't thank me. Gracias a Dios!...I gualmente.... Oh, gotta go. That's my other line....Hello?

INT. MAY LEE'S APARTMENT - MORNING

(Intercut, as needed)

A worried May paces, talks to Kathy on the phone.

> MAY
> How are you coming?

> KATHY
> Oh, you know. Tax time. I'm slammed. But I'll make it.

> MAY
> I need to speak with you about something.

> KATHY
> (off the unnatural sound in May's voice)
> Well, sure. Something the matter?

> MAY
> Look, I've got an extra ticket to the theater tonight. Why don't you join Marvin and me? We'll talk afterwards.

> KATHY
> You're such a good friend. You always throw me a life raft when I'm drowning. I could really use a break right now.

> MAY
> We're going to "Chuck Thaws Out."

                    KATHY
          God, I've been wanting to see that
          for ages.

                    MAY
          Eight o'clock. The Helen Hayes.
          Let's meet out in front.

                    KATHY
          Thank you so much, Con.

                    MAY
          What did you say?

                    KATHY
          I... I don't know. Thank you, I
          think.

                    MAY
          All right.

                    KATHY
          See you there.

INT. BRONX DRESS SHOP - DAY

Kathy hands a tax return to an exhausted MS. ORTIZ, 50s,
KIDS at her feet in the rundown establishment.

                    MS. ORTIZ
          Thank you, Kathy. I'll have your
          check soon.

                    KATHY
          Don't worry about it, Ms. Ortiz.

                    MS. ORTIZ
          I have to worry about it. I don't
          like being late like this. Next
          month. I promise. As soon as I get
          my refund.

                    KATHY
          Whenever you can.

                    MS. ORTIZ
          You are an angel.

INT. KATHY MURCER'S APARTMENT - EVENING

Her bed strewn with outfits, Kathy slips just the right one
on -- a lovely pink crepe de chine dress.

She picks up her purse and a small, gift-wrapped box and a
card addressed to May, heads to the door.

THE PHONE RINGS.

> KATHY
> Hello.

INT. MAY LEE'S APARTMENT

(Intercut, as needed)

> MAY
> Kathy.

> KATHY
> Sorry. I'm still here. I was just
> about to leave.

May stares at the letter from the IRS.

> KATHY (CONT'D)
> May? Are you still there?

> MAY
> I was wondering...

> KATHY
> Are you O.K.?

> MAY
> I was wondering if you...are you
> wearing the pink?

> KATHY
> Well, yes. God, how did you know
> that?

> MAY
> You look so lovely in it.
> I'll...I'll see you at the
> theater.

> KATHY
> I'm leaving right now.

> MAY
> Take a cab.

> KATHY
> The train's cheaper. I'll still
> make it. See you there.

          MAY
No. We'll pick you up. And that's
final.

Kathy hangs up. She looks at one of her plants. She picks
up a watering can, waters the plant, touches it lovingly.
May slams the phone down, rises, anguished -- martini in
hand -- walks to the windows. She watches the sun slip over
the horizon. The rosy night glow fades. She seems to turn
gray.

KNOCK AT THE DOOR. May manufactures a smile, answers it
slowly.

MARVIN SIMON, 40s, comes in. He's florid, rather in the
mold of Tweedle Dum or Tweedle Dee. Bald, mustachioed, he
wears a three-piece Italian suit with exaggerated
pinstripes the width of the foul lines at Yankee Stadium.
But his accent comes by way of Ebbetts Field.

Marvin, a good head shorter than May, takes her hands in
his sausage-like, perfectly manicured fingers, squeezes
them warmly.

          MARVIN
Hello, May.

          MAY
Marvin, dear. How's the rag
business?

          MARVIN
It's hell. But I prefer it to
heaven. How's the rug business?

          MAY
Great. Thanks to you. I think I'll
have to retire my "Customer of the
Month Award."

          MARVIN
Speaking of which.

Marvin peels off his toupee.

          MARVIN (CONT'D)
This one just wasn't...me.

          MAY
What is "you," then?

          [END EXERPT]

Stairs

by Jeff Williamson

Holocaust Memorial/Berlin, Germany

by Sarah Kayss

The Willing
(screenplay excerpt)

written by Phillip E. Hardy

"The Willing" is a feature-length screenplay by Phillip E. Hardy.

Phillip E. Hardy's screenplay is currently a Finalist at Creative Scope Awards and Quarter-Finalist at Screencraft Action/Thriller Competition. Hardy's previous screenplays have also received numerous awards.

TEXT ON SCREEN

"When cowardice is made respectable, its followers
are without number both from among the weak and the
strong."

                                        FADE IN:

INT. - BEDROOM - NIGHT

NEW HARTFORD, CONNECTICUT 1986

On a bleak winter night, snow falls outside a Victorian
home.

ERIC PILGRIM (13) glances out his window at the forest and
hears the sound of wolves howling nearby. He grabs a large
illustrated book off the shelf and jumps into bed with a
flashlight.

Eric leafs through pages of pictures. He stares at a
photograph of a young man and woman being hanged by Nazi
soldiers. He turns the page and intently looks at another
photo of a German officer shooting a man in the head. With
his flashlight, he reads the caption:

                "Killings, brutalities, cruelties,
                tortures, atrocities, medical
                experiments - inhuman acts were an
                everyday occurrence during the Nazi
                genocide."

                                        CUT TO:

EXT. - FOREST - MORNING

Eric, a lean teenager, is bundled up in camouflage hunting
clothes. He quietly walks along a wooded path covered with
a thin layer of snow. In his arms, he cradles a Winchester
30/30 rifle.

As he passes through a thicket, Eric sees a GREY WOLF on
the pathway about twenty five yards in front of him. He
halts and the two earthly creatures stare at one another
for several seconds.

The Wolf bounds towards the young man.

Eric calmly holds his ground. And aims his rifle at the
oncoming beast.

The wolf leaps at his prey.

GUNSHOT

Eric shoots the wolf in midair.

YELPING SOUND

The wolf lands on its side, on the cold ground with a
bullet in its chest.

Eric walks over to the wounded animal and stands above it.

> ERIC PILGRIM
> (looking down)
> Survival of the fittest.

Lifting his heavy hiking boot, Eric crushes the wolf's
skull. He pulls out a hunting knife, stoops down and begins
cutting off the wolf's left paw.

CUT TO:

INT. - BEDROOM - NIGHT

Eric reads another book about the Nazi regime. He scans a
passage:

> "At Auschwitz, several camp
> physicians performed experiments
> that included castration, freezing
> and drowning human beings."

Eric underlines the word drowning.

CUT TO:

EXT. - BACKYARD - DAY

Eric carries a small cage containing FERDINAND, a white
rat.

He sets it down, walks over to the deck and grabs a mop
bucket and places it near the end of a garden hose. He
opens a notebook and writes the following.

> May 28th: I am performing my
> experiment on Ferdinand to see how
> long he can tread water.

Eric puts Ferdinand inside the bucket and rapidly begins
filling it with water.

Ferdinand begins frantically treading around the sides and
scratching at the edge of the plastic bucket.

Eric starts writing notes and then starts to giggle.

ANDREW PILGRIM (38) silently walks up behind his teenage son.

BOOMING VOICE

                ANDREW PILGRIM
        What in heaven's name are you
        doing?

                ERIC PILGRIM
        (startled)
        Just a little experiment.

Andrew leans down and grabs Ferdinand out of the bucket. He dries him off with his shirt sleeve and gingerly puts him back inside his cage.

                ANDREW PILGRIM
        That has to be one of the cruelest
        things I've ever seen anyone ever
        do.

                ERIC PILGRIM
        I was going to pull him out before
        he drowned.

                ANDREW PILGRIM
        Son, a rat can tread water for
        hours, maybe days.
        (beat)
        Ferdinand is your pet. Why do want
        to see him suffer?

                ERIC PILGRIM
        I didn't know how long he could
        tread water. I wanted to see for
        myself.

                ANDREW PILGRIM
        (disgusted)
        Good god boy. In the future, you
        better fulfill your curiosity in
        other ways.

                                  CUT TO:

INT. - OFFICE - DAY

Bespectacled Doctor, BARRY SPURLING (42) sits in a big
leather chair in his office with note pad in hand.

Eric Pilgrim sits back on a reclining office chair with his
arms folded tightly.

> DOCTOR SPURLING
> Eric, do you know why you're here?

> ERIC PILGRIM
> I dunno, why don't you tell me
> Doctor Mengele?

> DOCTOR SPURLING
> Doctor Mengele?
> (chuckles)
> As a Jew, I ought to take offense
> by that remark. He was a pretty
> nasty customer, don't you think?

> ERIC PILGRIM
> I read that his work probably
> saved a lot of German soldiers and
> that he contracted typhus working
> with Jewish patients at Auschwitz.

> DOCTOR SPURLING
> Well, we're not here to debate the
> merits of Doctor Mengele's work.
> We're here to talk about you.

> ERIC PILGRIM
> My favorite subject.

> DOCTOR SPURLING
> You didn't answer my question.

> ERIC PILGRIM
> Refresh my memory.

> DOCTOR SPURLING
> Why do you think your parents
> brought you in?

> ERIC PILGRIM
> (leans forward)
> I suppose my dad thinks I'm a sicko
> for putting Ferdinand in a water
> bucket.

                    DOCTOR SPURLING
Do you think you're a sicko?

                    ERIC PILGRIM
No, I'm a scientist.

                    DOCTOR SPURLING
Then as a scientist, why did you
try to drown Ferdinand?

                    ERIC PILGRIM
I wasn't going to let him drown. I
wanted to see how long he could
tread water.

                    DOCTOR SPURLING
To what end? Does tormenting a
helpless animal give you sense of
power. a sense of control?

                    ERIC PILGRIM
Is that what they teach you in
Freud's clown college?

                    DOCTOR SPURLING
  (smiles)
I'm not a traditional Freudian or
behavioral psychologist. I'm a
client centered therapist.

                    ERIC PILGRIM
Are we going to hold hands and get
in touch with our feelings?

                    DOCTOR SPURLING
No, and I'm not going to kiss you
either. I'm here to create a non
judgmental environment where you
can discuss any adverse or negative
stuff that may keep you from having
a positive life.

                    ERIC PILGRIM
  (giggles)
Alright Doc.

                    DOCTOR SPURLING
What are you laughing about?

                    ERIC PILGRIM
        I'm still processing the part where
        you said you won't kiss me. What,
        I'm not good enough for you?

                    DOCTOR SPURLING
        Let's cut the bullshit son. I've
        reviewed your Stanford Binet scores
        and they're off the charts. All
        your teachers say you're very
        gifted. Some say even a genius.

                    ERIC PILGRIM
              (mocking voice)
        Eric's very smart. But he just doesn't apply
        himself.
              (beat)
        So, you've been checking up on me?

                    DOCTOR SPURLING
        Your folks are rather concerned
        about your recent proclivities.

                    ERIC PILGRIM
        All because I gave my rat a bath?

                    DOCTOR SPURLING
        Your father said you shot a wolf
        and then smashed its head in.

                    ERIC PILGRIM
        Maybe my old man forgot to tell
        you. That wolf tried to kill me.

                    DOCTOR SPURLING
        Look, I don't want to spend weeks,
        months or years getting to know you.

                    ERIC PILGRIM
        Amen to that.

                    DOCTOR SPURLING
        I think I have an idea that might
        illustrate why the path you're
        taking may lead you to trouble down
        the road.

                    ERIC PILGRIM
        How so?

                    DOCTOR SPURLING
          Have you ever heard of Ed Gein?

                    ERIC PILGRIM
          No, who is he?

                    DOCTOR SPURLING
          He's a little before your time.
          But why don't we watch a video I
          have about him.

                    ERIC PILGRIM
               (shrugs)
          Why not.

Spurling gets up, turns on his television and pops a tape
into the VCR.

The television reveals the character of LEATHERFACE, who
chases a girl out of a barn.

                    NARRATOR
               (over television)
          He was a grave robber that lived in
          unimaginable squalor.

The television reveals the character of NORMAN BATES.

                    NARRATOR (CONT'D)
               (over television)
          Leatherface from Texas Chain Saw
          Massacre and Norman Bates from
          Psycho are based on his life.

The television reveals an unfamiliar face on the screen.

                    NARRATOR (CONT'D)
               (over television)
          His name was Ed Gein, a seemingly
          mild mannered Wisconsin farmer.

The television reveals black and white images of a small
community with mom and pop shops and old cars.

                    NARRATOR (CONT'D)
               (over television)
          His degenerate activities may have
          gone unnoticed but for one fateful
          weekend in the fall of 1958.

The television reveals men in the forest hunting and then we see a man butchering a carcass.

>   NARRATOR (CONT'D)
>   (over television)
>   It was the beginning of deer
>   season. And the men of Plainfield
>   were all out in the woods hunting.

The television reveals a picture of an ancient storefront.

>   NARRATOR (CONT'D)
>   (over television)
>   This left Bernice Worden's hardware
>   store nearly empty, except for one
>   particular customer who had another
>   type of game in mind.

The television reveals a reenactment of two officers fumbling around with flashlights in a dark wooden building.

>   NARRATOR (CONT'D)
>   (over television)
>   Deputies found Worden's headless
>   corpse naked and butchered, hanging
>   upside down in Ed Gein's wood shed.

The television reveals images of various body parts and other macabre items.

>   NARRATOR (CONT'D)
>   (over television)
>   A ghastly array of things including
>   bowls made from human skulls,
>   chairs, lamp shades made from human
>   skin and flayed heads fashioned
>   into face masks decorated his home.

Eric's eyes widen with fascination at the gruesome account of the killer's home inventory.

The television reveals a lurid photograph of distorted face.

>   NARRATOR (CONT'D)
>   (over television)
>   One officer found a brown bag with
>   the face of a female victim named
>   Mary Hogan, who had gone missing
>   three years earlier.

Doctor Spurling turns off the television.

              DOCTOR SPURLING
So, what do you think of Ed Gein?

              ERIC PILGRIM
What a freak show.

              DOCTOR SPURLING
Yes, his poor sleepy hometown
became a media circus. And people
wondered how a psychopath like that
was created.

              ERIC PILGRIM
How was he created Doc?

              DOCTOR SPURLING
He liked a lot of things that you
like.

              ERIC PILGRIM
   (rolls eyes)
Like what?

              DOCTOR SPURLING
He liked killing small animals. He
liked picture books about Nazis. He
was a lone wolf like you. He liked
trophies from his victims too.

              ERIC PILGRIM
What do you mean?

              DOCTOR SPURLING
Your father found a wolf's paw in
your dresser drawer.

              ERIC PILGRIM
So.

              DOCTOR SPURLING
Did you cut it off the one you shot?

              ERIC PILGRIM
What if I did?

              DOCTOR SPURLING
Isn't that a trophy?

                ERIC PILGRIM
I wanted something to remember him
by.

                DOCTOR SPURLING
Let me change the subject a bit. Do
you like girls?

                ERIC PILGRIM
Of course I like them.

                DOCTOR SPURLING
Well that's something you don't
have in common with Ed. With the
exception of his mother, he thought
all women were strumpets.

                ERIC PILGRIM
You mean whores?

                DOCTOR SPURLING
Yes.

                ERIC PILGRIM
Jeez, what a nut bucket.

                DOCTOR SPURLING
Do you think about girls a lot?

                ERIC PILGRIM
Yes. There's one at school named
Anne Jensen that I'd love to nail.

                DOCTOR SPURLING
You're thirteen, so I'm assuming
you've never seen a girl naked.

                ERIC PILGRIM
In Playboy magazine.

                DOCTOR SPURLING
Look son, if you ever want to have
a girlfriend and get laid, you need
to change your path.

                ERIC PILGRIM
What do you mean?

                                [END EXCERPT]

'We Govern We' by Mulligan's Island (stills)

music video directed by Jeffrey Blake Palmer

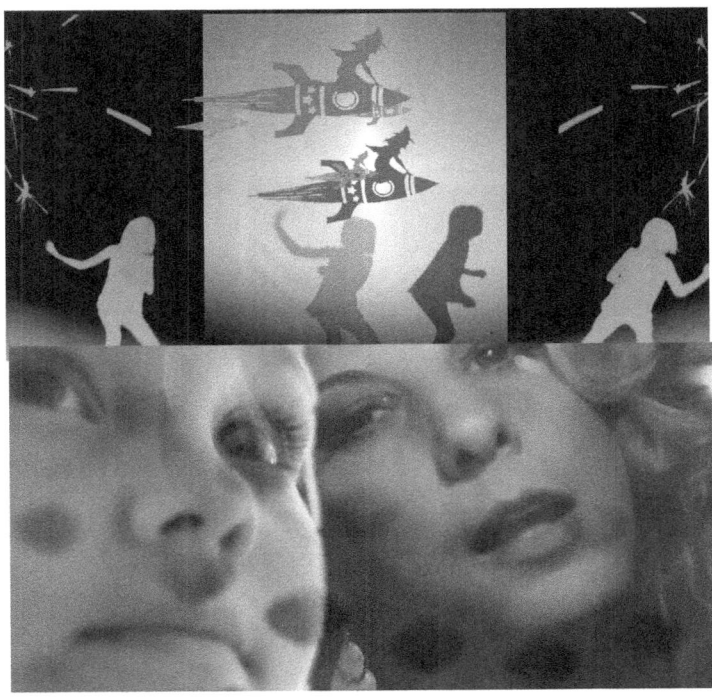

Strings
(screenplay excerpt)

written by Peter Wisan

"Strings" is a feature-length screenplay by Peter Wisan.

Peter has an extensive background in creative writing. He has been published in the Marine Corps Gazette. Peter also worked as a script reader in both a production company and in screenplay competitions. He has several feature films, tv pilots, and short films under a wide array of genres.

EXT. CITY - DAY

Post-apocalyptic, futuristic dystopian scenes: Cities
fashioned of rubble. Concrete dust thick in the air.
Garbage can fires.

An aged man, BRAMMEL DORL, speaks.

>   BRAMMEL V.O.
>   So this is the future...
>   The scene fades away.

INT. ROOM - DAY

The dorm of any student--except the technology is
futuristic. Though new to us, it's very well-worn.

A TEENAGER is playing a tarnished clarinet. On a large
monitor in front cf him is a very old teacher, Brammel
Dorl.

The computer image is intentionally blurred and pixelated.

>   BRAMMEL
>   Play the last phrase. But with
>   feeling.

The kid butchers a couple measures.

BEEP! A text box appears: Five minutes remaining.

>   BRAMMEL (CONT'D)
>   I think that's enough for today.

INT. BRAMMEL'S CABIN - DAY

A cozy log cabin, bare and rough. One corner has a large
computer monitor. Brammel shuts off his screen, which has a
similar blurry video of the teenager on it. He rubs his
eyes wearily.

>   BRAMMEL
>   I've lived too long. Too many
>   musical butchers.

>   TEENAGER O.S.
>   Your mic's still on.

Brammel pulls the cord to his computer. It zaps off.

Brammel plods over to a rolltop desk. He pulls out a
DICTAJOURNAL (a small, personal recorder, a quarter the
width of a
card deck).

>   BRAMMEL
>   Dicta-journal initiate. June 5th.
>   Student 1-7-3-x-zed-50 makes slow,
>   slow progress.
>   (a beat)
>   Possibly reverse progress. Am
>   holding breath for coming semester
>   and the new crop of "students".

He puts down the recorder and meanders past a chessboard.
He moves a piece in passing.

He continues to a window. Outside a deer cautiously chews
leaves off a tree.

>   BRAMMEL (CONT'D)
>   (to deer)
>   A college teacher? Why? Oh, that's
>   right. I'd almost forgotten.
>   Because I can't do anything else.
>   Thanks, deer-

He twinkles slightly at the pun. The deer looks up.

>   BRAMMEL (CONT'D)
>   --You always know just what to say.

INT. BRAMMEL'S CABIN - NIGHT

Brammel reads in bed. Another dull night. He sighs.

The book falls from his hands. Brammel stares out the
window. He shrugs and turns off the light.

EXT. BRAMMEL'S CABIN - DAY

A cabin nestled in the clearing of an idyllic pine forest.

Birds chirp. Light beams shaft boldly through the dense
foliage.

INT. BRAMMEL'S CABIN - DAY

Brammel sits at his computer. A different blurred person
hovers on the screen: His brother, GRAIN DORL (82).

                    BRAMMEL
--Oh, no, their minds are passé
and unfortunate. Like a zoo
without animals. Seemingly bent on
destroying music. How are your art
students?

                    GRAIN
Their works show great range and
color.

                    BRAMMEL
That's not what I asked. How are
the students?

                    GRAIN
Let's not do this.

                    BRAMMEL
Do you remember when college wasn't
entirely online? When the world
wasn't so...technical? Wasn't that
grand?

                    GRAIN
It's not wise to speak of this.
It's even imprudent for us to talk
so frequently.

                    BRAMMEL
The law says people may speak
virtually whenever and as often as
they like! In fact, it's encouraged.

                    GRAIN
I know what it says. But not
family. You know that.

                    BRAMMEL
That's not in the law.

                    GRAIN
Some things don't have to be
written to be laws.

                    BRAMMEL
We haven't spoken in three years!

                    GRAIN
I'm sorry.

Brammel sighs.

>   BRAMMEL
>   Are we just a couple of old fools?

>   GRAIN
>   That's probably the smartest thing
>   you've said in years, brother.

>   BRAMMEL
>   What if we were... to meet up?

>   GRAIN
>   If that was a joke, it wasn't
>   funny. I should go.

>   BRAMMEL
>   I didn't mean it.

>   GRAIN
>   'Til next time.

Grain disappears from the screen. Brammel doesn't move from
the half-light.

>   BRAMMEL
>   See you in three years.

EXT. CITY - DAY

CAIRA, 25, uniquely beautiful, walks the city streets. A
young couple approaches: SHARP (male) and VEENA (female).
Caira is shocked to see them hand-in-hand. They look at her
and laugh carelessly.

She averts their gaze instantly, reflexively. Caira passes
them as quickly as possible. Yet she looks back. She checks
herself and quickens her pace.

INT. BRAMMEL'S CABIN -DAY

Brammel prepares a sandwich. His computer BEEPS as a text
box appears: "New Student. Session Initiating."

Brammel is too deep in thought to notice.

A blurry JOSIAH KARICK (18) appears on the screen. He holds
a violin. His mind functions at an eight-year old level.

>   JOSIAH
>   Hello? Is anybody there?

Brammel is yanked rudely from his daydreams.

He hesitates, putting off the musical torture as long as possible.

> JOSIAH (CONT'D)
> Hello?

Brammel gives in.

> BRAMMEL
> Ah, yes. Here. Are you ready to be the death of an old man?

> JOSIAH
> I don't understand.

> BRAMMEL
> Never mind. Just go ahead. Play up to the A-6. But with feeling.

> JOSIAH
> I don't know what that means.

> BRAMMEL
> Of course not. Just start playing, I suppose.

Brammel pours himself a drink. He wanders absentmindedly.

Beautiful, slow vibrato notes bleed from the computer.

Brammel freezes. His glass shatters on the floor.

> BRAMMEL (CONT'D)
> (under his breath)
> If you can do that with a simple arpeggio, think what you could accomplish with a real piece of music.

A tear rolls down Brammel's cheek. PLOP on the glass shards.

[END EXCERPT]